Spring into Summer!

Adapted by Tish Rabe
from a script by Karen Moonah
Illustrated by Aristides Ruiz and Joe Mathieu

Random House 🏠 New York

Based in part on *The Cat in the Hat Knows a Lot About That!* TV series (Episode 140) © CITH Productions, Inc. (a subsidiary of Portfolio Entertainment, Inc.), and Red Hat Animation, Ltd. (a subsidiary of Collingwood O'Hare Productions, Ltd.), 2010–2011.

THE CAT IN THE HAT KNOWS A LOT ABOUT THAT! logo and word mark TM 2010 Dr. Seuss Enterprises, L.P., Portfolio Entertainment, Inc., and Collingwood O'Hare Productions, Ltd. All rights reserved. The PBS KIDS logo is a registered trademark of PBS. Both are used with permission. All rights reserved.

Broadcast in Canada by Treehouse™. Treehouse™ is a trademark of the Corus® Entertainment Inc. group of companies. All rights reserved.

Visit us on the Web! Seussville.com pbskids.org/catinthehat treehousetv.com
Educators and librarians, for a variety of teaching tools, visit us at www.randomhouse.com/teachers
ISBN: 978-0-307-93057-6   Library of Congress Control Number: 2011925074
MANUFACTURED IN CHINA   10 9 8 7 6 5 4

"Our tree house is great,"
said Nick. "We play here
with all types of toys
different times of the year.

Spring, summer, fall, winter,
we have such great fun.
Sally, which season is
your favorite one?"

"I'm not sure," Sally said.
"I like spring, oh, I do.
But I also like summer
and I know you do, too."

"Did someone say *seasons*?"
the Cat asked. "Let's ride
to a palace of ice with
a garden inside!

To the Garden of Seasons!
It's where you will meet
my good friend Gardenia.
She's wise and she's sweet.

She knows about seasons,
and she will show you
all four of the seasons
before she is through!"

"Gardenia," the Cat said,
"meet Sally and Nick."
"Hello!" said Gardenia.
"I'll show you a trick.

All four of the seasons
are here to explore.
You will walk into spring
when you open this door."

"Welcome to spring!"
said a brown snowshoe hare.
"My name is Sam.
I live right over there."

Then they heard a *honk*
and Nick asked, "What's that?"
"I know what that is,"
said the Cat in the Hat.

"That is a honk
that's unlike any other. . . ."

"It's Candy the Gosling,
who's here with her mother."

"See those fish," said Nick,
"hiding under those logs?"
"We're not fish," one piped up.
"We are baby frogs.

We are called tadpoles
and soon, it's no joke,
we will turn into frogs and
you'll hear us all croak!"

"I'm Woody," he said.
"I'm a wood frog, you see.
In a couple of months,
you won't recognize me!"

"I like spring," said Sally,
"but let's fly away,
then come back to this place
on a hot summer's day!"

"Spring's nice," said Gardenia.
"But summer is, too.
See for yourself through
this door that is blue."

"It's summer!" said Sally.
"And I can tell why.
It's hot—and the sun is
up high in the sky."

"Hello there!" said Sam.
"I'm glad you are here.
Summer's my most favorite
time of the year."

"Hello!" someone croaked.
"I'm so glad to see you!"
A fully grown wood frog
then hopped into view.

"Woody!" said Nick.
"You've grown up since spring!"
"Now hopping," said Woody,
"is my favorite thing."

Then they heard some loud honking.
The Cat started to shout:
"Incoming! Everyone—
get down and watch out!"

"It's Candy!" said Sally.
Nick said, "Is that true?
You've gotten so big.
Is that really you?"

"In spring," said the Cat,
"plants and animals sprout.
By summer they're bigger.
Frogs now leap about.

Which season's your favorite?"
Then Sally said, "Well . . .
we've seen spring and summer
but it's hard to tell.

In spring babies grow,
and in summer it's hot.
I think I like both spring and
summer . . ."

"So, Nick," said the Cat.
"Tell us, what do you think
about winter, now that we
have our own skating rink?"

"Winter's great!" said Nick.
"But fall's lots of fun.
It's too hard to pick
a favorite one!"

"You're right," said the Cat.
"But I'll give you good news.
Each season is fun
and we don't have to choose."

"Spring and summer," said Sally,
"winter and fall.
Which season's our favorite?
Well, we like . . ."

When fall becomes winter,
his fur becomes white,
which blends in with the snow,
where he hides out of sight."

"Where's Woody?" asked Sally.
"I don't see him here."
"Woody sleeps," said the Cat,
"at this time of the year.

Wood frogs hibernate
under leaves, winter through.
If you were a wood frog,
you'd hibernate, too.

Now I can't wait.
The cold air is so nice.
It's time to go skating.
Let's take to the ice!"

"Welcome back!" a voice said.
And Nick asked, "Who's there?"
"It's me, your friend Sam,"
said a white snowshoe hare.

"Cat . . . ," whispered Nick.
"Is our friend Sam all right?
His fur used to be brown
and now it's all white."

"Not to worry!" the Cat said.
"It may strike you as strange,
but hares such as Sam
have brown fur that will change.

"Winter," said Gardenia,
"is filled with delight.
To see it, just pass through
this door that is white."

"I like fall," said Nick,
"but I'd like to know
what this place will look like
when it's covered in snow.

Let's go ask Gardenia.
We can leave right away—
and come back again
on a cold winter's day."

"There goes Candy the Goose!"
Sally said. "She told me
she flies south in the fall
with her whole family."

"It's true," said the Cat.
"In the fall, the geese go
to a place where it's warm
before winter winds blow."

"Goodbye!" Candy called.
"Yes, it's time to take wing.
But I'll see you folks soon.
I'll be back in the spring!"

They made a big pile,
and in less than a minute
their friends Sam and Woody-
began to jump in it!

Then they heard honking
and looked up to see
geese flying on high
in the shape of a "V."

"It's fall and the leaves
have changed color," Nick said.
"They were green. Now they're
yellow and orange and red!"

"Fall leaves," said the Cat,
"are perfect, I know,
for leaf leaping! Come on—
let's get ready, set, GO!"

"If it's fall," said Gardenia,
"that you wish to know,
then through this red door
is the way you should go."

"Fall and winter!" the Cat cried.
"Those seasons are great!
In fall, we carve pumpkins!
In winter, we skate!"

"I like carving pumpkins
and skating," said Nick.
"Which season's my favorite—
and how do I pick?"

"I know," said the Cat,
"who can help you to choose.
To the Garden of Seasons!
There's no time to lose!

Gardenia will show us
both winter and fall
and help Nick to pick
his favorite season of all!"

"Sally," said Nick,
"we fly kites in the spring,
and swimming in summer is
my favorite thing.

I love spring and summer.
There's so much to do.
But the fall and the winter
are lots of fun, too."

Fall into Winter!

Adapted by Tish Rabe
from a script by Karen Moonah
Illustrated by Aristides Ruiz and Joe Mathieu

Random House 🏠 New York

TM and copyright © by Dr. Seuss Enterprises, L.P. 2012. All rights reserved. Published in the United States by Random House Children's Books, a division of Random House, Inc., 1745 Broadway, New York, NY 10019. Random House and the colophon are registered trademarks of Random House, Inc.

Based in part on *The Cat in the Hat Knows a Lot About That!* TV series (Episode 140) © CITH Productions, Inc. (a subsidiary of Portfolio Entertainment, Inc.), and Red Hat Animation, Ltd. (a subsidiary of Collingwood O'Hare Productions, Ltd.), 2010–2011.

THE CAT IN THE HAT KNOWS A LOT ABOUT THAT! logo and word mark TM 2010 Dr. Seuss Enterprises, L.P., Portfolio Entertainment, Inc., and Collingwood O'Hare Productions, Ltd. All rights reserved. The PBS KIDS logo is a registered trademark of PBS. Both are used with permission. All rights reserved.

Broadcast in Canada by Treehouse™. Treehouse™ is a trademark of the Corus® Entertainment Inc. group of companies. All rights reserved.

Visit us on the Web!   Seussville.com   pbskids.org/catinthehat   treehousetv.com
Educators and librarians, for a variety of teaching tools, visit us at www.randomhouse.com/teachers
ISBN: 978-0-307-93057-6   Library of Congress Control Number: 2011925074
MANUFACTURED IN CHINA   10 9 8 7 6 5 4